Fresh & Fun

February

BY JOAN NOVELLI

SCHOLASTIC
PROFESSIONAL **B**OOKS

NEW YORK • TORONTO • LONDON • AUCKLAND • SYDNEY
MEXICO CITY • NEW DELHI • HONG KONG

For Diane Farnham, who inspired the take-home activity calendars
featured in this and other <u>Fresh & Fun Month-by-Month</u> books—
and for being the teacher my son remembers as "the best teacher in the world."

Many thanks to the creative teachers who contributed ideas to this book:
Peg Arcadi, Jan Armstrong Freitag, Rita Galloway, Bob Krech, Sue Lorey, Mary Modoono, Frank Murphy,
Deirdre Parkhurst, Natalie Vaughan, Lori Vig, and Nicole Vig.

"Hide-and-Seek Shadow" by Margaret Hillert from FARTHER THAN FAR. Copyright © 1969 by Follett Publishing Co.
Used by permission of the author, who controls all rights.

Produced by Joan Novelli
Front cover, interior, and poster design by Kathy Massaro
Cover and interior art by Shelley Dieterichs, except page 11 by James Graham Hale
Poster art by Anne Kennedy

ISBN 0-439-21605-2
Copyright © 2000 by Joan Novelli
Printed in the U.S.A.
All rights reserved.

Contents

The month of February may bring more winter to many of us—but it also comes with a wealth of teaching opportunities. February 2nd invites stories of groundhogs forecasting the weather—and explorations into whatever weather is happening around you. Children's excitement for Valentine's Day starts building long before February 14th rolls around, and, of course, everyone looks forward to Presidents' Day—a time to celebrate our nation's leaders (and for many to have a day off!). February is also Dental Health Month, making it a great time to investigate teeth—a topic full of interdisciplinary connections.

This book is designed to make it easy for you to integrate these topics into your teaching. It's divided into four sections—one for each topic (GROUNDHOG DAY/SHADOWS, VALENTINE'S DAY, PRESIDENTS, and TEETH). Activities for each topic connect every corner of your curriculum—from reading and writing to science, movement, music, and art. Many of the activities naturally integrate several disciplines. For example, "Counting on Presidents" combines math and history as children learn about money and the presidents whose pictures appear on it. (See page 19.) "What Big Teeth!" combines math and science as children discover surprising facts about animal friends. (See page 28.) "Rock-a-Bye Shadow" brings science and music together in an easy-to-learn song about light and shadows. (See page 9.) Special features in the book include:

♡ a reproducible send-home activity calendar

♡ computer connections

♡ hands-on math and science activities

♡ literature connections

♡ collaborative bookmaking projects

♡ an easy-to-learn "piggyback" song

♡ ready-to-use reproducible activity pages

♡ a reproducible mini-book to make

♡ no-cook snacks to make and enjoy

♡ a reproducible mini-play

♡ a rhyming collaborative banner

♡ a colorful poetry poster to display, plus a four-week lesson plan

♡ and much more February fun!

TIP

Throughout this book, you'll find web site suggestions to support various activities. Please remember that Internet locations and contents can change over time. We cannot guarantee the availability of sites recommended in this book at the time of publication.

Multiple Intelligences Connections

Your students learn in different ways—some are more verbal, others prefer written expression. Some are comfortable working in groups, others like independent projects. Some children's strengths lie in music, art, and other modes of expression. To help you meet your students' needs and encourage all of their strengths, you'll find all these learning modalities woven into the activities in this book.

Name _____

February Activity Calendar

Choose _____ activities to do each week this month.
Ask an adult in your family to initial the square in the box of each activity
you complete. Bring this paper back to school on _____ .

Monday	Tuesday	Wednesday	Thursday	Friday
Write the word *February* on a sheet of paper. Cut apart the letters. Make new words! **are bear far**	Look at a calendar. Count the days in February. Are there any other months with the same number of days?	Look at this heart. Find a matching heart on this page.	Find Presidents' Day on a calendar. How many days in February come before Presidents' Day? after?	Look at some coins. Which coins have pictures of President Lincoln and President Washington on them?
Who is the president of our country? Tell what you know about this person.	Tell five things you'd like the president to do to make this country better. What can you do to help your country?	How many pennies in a quarter? Which is worth more: 75 pennies or 4 quarters?	Look at a calendar. Find a month that has four of the same letters as February.	*Be mine.* List as many words as you can that have the word *be* in them. **belong because maybe**
Unscramble these words to make a Valentine message: **Valentine you mine be will**	What is red? Make a list of things that are red. You've made a list poem! Give your poem a title.	Go outside with an adult in your family. Can you make your shadows hold hands even when you're not?	Use a flashlight to make shadows of objects. What's the tallest shadow you can make? shortest? widest?	Look at pictures in a newspaper with a family member. Tell a story about what you see.
It's Dental Health Month! Make a blank calendar. Give yourself a star each time you brush your teeth.	Listen to the ending sound of the word *teeth*. Take turns with a family member naming words that begin with or end in *th*.	Some sharks can grow 2,000 teeth in one year! Count your teeth. How many more does a shark have?	Put water in two plastic cups. Sprinkle salt in one. Put the cups in the freezer. Which do you think will freeze first?	Turn *February* into a tongue twister! Make up a sentence using as many words as you can that start with f.

Fresh & Fun February Scholastic Professional Books

5

Teaching With the Poster: "Hide-and-Seek Shadow"

Playing with shadows is as much a part of childhood as taking those first steps. Use children's natural fascination for shadows to learn more.

Week 1: Walk, Run, and Dance

Let children play with their shadows like the child in the poem. Take children outside on a sunny day and read the poem aloud slowly. Have them vary their movement with each of the first three lines—walking, running, then dancing with their shadows. Can they make their shadows hide?

Week 2: Pocket Chart Play

Copy each line of the poem on a sentence strip. Cut apart each word. Place the words in order line by line on the pocket chart. Read the poem with children, then take out the words *walked*, *ran*, and *danced*. Ask: *How are these words alike?* (They tell something you do. They are "action" words, or *verbs*.) Ask children to suggest other words that tell how they could play with their shadows—for example, *skipped*, *jumped*, and *wiggled*. Write their words on sentence strips and trim. Read the poem again and again, letting children substitute new words each time for *walked*, *ran*, and *danced*.

Week 3: What Makes a Shadow?

Invite children to name all of the things in the poster that make shadows. Ask: *Where is the sun in this picture?* Guide students to recognize that a shadow is made when an object blocks light. Give children flashlights to use in small groups. Dim the lights and let them experiment with shining the flashlight on assorted objects to make shadows. *Can they make a long shadow? a short shadow? a wide shadow? a skinny shadow?*

Week 4: Celebrating Shadows

Plan a week of shadow games.

◎ Play "Shadow Tag." Children tag one another by stepping on their shadows. Get students thinking by asking: *What is the best way to avoid being tagged—running into or away from the sun?* (If they run away from the sun, their shadows will be in front of them and easier to keep track of!)

◎ Play "Shadow Me!" Pair up children. Have them take turns making movements for their partners to copy like a shadow.

◎ No hands! Can children make their shadows hold hands without holding hands themselves? Have children stand in a circle. Can they make their shadows form a star or flower shape?

TIP

Caution children not to look directly at the sun.

Book Break

Light and Shadow

(Scholastic, 1996)

This *I Can Read About Science* book uses poems to introduce concepts related to the sun, rainbows, shadows, and more.

Teacher Share

MOVEMENT, SCIENCE

What Do You See, Groundhog?

Celebrate Groundhog Day and introduce an investigation of shadows with this movement activity. Make a simple groundhog mask by taping ears to a construction-paper headband. Invite a volunteer to be the "groundhog" and put on the ears. Have the other children line up front to back with legs apart to make a tunnel or "burrow." Give the first child in line a flashlight. Have the groundhog go to the back of the burrow and crawl through. When the groundhog sticks his or her head out, what will it see? The first child can choose whether or not to shine the light on the groundhog to make a shadow. Have the groundhog go back in the burrow if he or she sees its shadow, or crawl all the way out if there's no shadow. Play again, letting children take turns being the groundhog.

Nicole Vig
Nuttin' But Kids Preschool
Green Bay, Wisconsin

TIP

What is another name for a groundhog? Challenge children to find out! (*woodchuck*)

Book Break

The Story of Punxsutawney Phil, the Fearless Forecaster

by Julia Spencer Moutran (Crown, 1977)

Phil helps his family get ready for winter, settles in for a long nap, then pops out of his burrow on Groundhog Day to predict the weather. Just how reliable is that forecast? Share this surprising story to find out.

Teacher Share

Groundhogs and Other Ways to Predict Weather

After letting children discuss the possibility of a groundhog predicting weather, share other examples of weather lore—for example, *When sheep gather in a huddle, we'll soon have a puddle*. Write these sayings on chart paper, then let children pair up for some weather-forecasting fun. Have them either copy and illustrate one of the sayings on the chart paper, or come up with an original bit of weather lore. For children who want to write their own, the *Scholastic Rhyming Dictionary* by Sue Young will come in handy. These illustrated examples of weather lore make an interesting display that will spark lots of discussions.

Lori Vig
Varnum Elementary School
Lowell, Massachusetts

Groundhog Shadow Play

Explore light and shadow with the groundhog puppets on page 11. Let each child choose a groundhog pattern to color and cut out. (Glue to tagboard first.) Have children glue their groundhogs to craft sticks. Darken the room and give each pair of students a flashlight. Have them work together to make shadows. Can children with small groundhogs make shadows that are bigger than those of the large groundhogs? To do this, they will have to experiment with the placement of their groundhog and the light. (*Moving the groundhog closer to the light makes it bigger. Moving it away makes it smaller.*) Follow up by letting children share their findings. This is a good opportunity for science journal writing.

SCIENCE, ART

Silhouette Shows

Many students are familiar with the standard silhouette—a framed profile of someone in shadow. To make a silhouette, light is projected on a person's profile, and the resulting shadow on the wall is traced on dark paper. This shape is cut out and mounted on light-colored paper. Demonstrate the procedure for children, then invite them to create silhouette shows in small groups. Have students plan their cast of characters, then draw and cut out outlines of each. Have them tape their cutouts to craft sticks or straws, then practice their shows. To create shadows (or silhouettes), they'll need to project light on a wall and hold their puppets in between the light and the wall. For Silhouette Show ideas, see Tip, right.

TIP

Suggestions for silhouette shows include:

◎ Dramatize a favorite children's book. (Make silhouettes of the characters and related props.)

◎ Act out a groundhog popping out of its tunnel on Groundhog Day: *What does it see? What happens?*

◎ Act out an original story.

Teacher Share

MUSIC, SCIENCE

Rock-a-Bye Shadow

Introduce and explore concepts of light and shadow with this gentle rhyming song, sung to the familiar tune of "Rock-a-Bye Baby."

After singing the song several times, try these activities to learn more.

◎ Use a flashlight to simulate the sun, making tall and short shadows by changing the position of the "sun" in the sky.

◎ Look for rhyming words in the song—such as *small, tall, wall.* Use them to reinforce word families.

◎ Listen for opposites in the song—for example, *big/small, higher/shorter,* and *far/near.* Invite children to suggest other opposites. Record them on sentence strips, mix them up, and place in a pocket chart. Let children move the words around to match opposites.

Rock-a-Bye Shadow

I make a shadow, big or small.
When the day starts, my shadow is tall.
The higher the sun, the shorter it gets.
My shadow is gone, when the sun sets.

I make a shadow on the wall.
When the light's far, my shadow is tall.
When the light's near, my shadow grows long.
And when the light's off, my shadow is gone.

Peg Arcadi
Homeschool Teacher
Trumansburg, New York

Book Break

I Spy Mystery

by Jean Marzollo (Scholastic, 1993)

Display the picture on pages 12 and 13 of this popular picture riddle book. Ask: *What direction do you think the light is coming from to make these shadows?* Let children experiment with a flashlight and objects in the classroom to discover the answer. Go on to look for peculiar things in the picture. For example, are there shadows that don't have objects with them? What might be making them? Find the monster face shadow. What objects were used to make it? Experiment with objects in the classroom to make other funny shadow faces.

Teacher Share

MATH, SCIENCE

Standing in My Footsteps

Explore the relationship of the sun's position to shadow size with this "foots-on" activity.

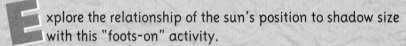

◎ Take children outside on a sunny day to a safe, empty paved area. Have them partner up to trace one another's feet on the pavement. (Provide chalk.) Have them stand in their footprints while their partners trace their shadows. Do this early in the day, if possible. Note the position of the sun. (Remind children not to look directly at the sun.)

◎ Take children outside to the same spot several more times during the day. Have them stand in their footsteps while their partners trace their shadows. (You might provide different-colored chalk each time.) Note the position of the sun each time.

◎ At the end of the day, compare the length of the different shadows. Guide children in making a connection between the time of day, the sun's position, and the length of their shadows. Ask: *Where was the sun when your shadow was longest? shortest? What time tomorrow do you think you would see the longest shadow? shortest?*

Natalie Vaughan
Phoenix School
Encinitas, California

Groundhog Shadow Play

TIP

This is a fun activity for any month. Just look for a seasonal connection when choosing the class "gift" that will go inside the box. Children will look forward to this activity from one month to the next. Watch their writing skills grow as they write about what they think is inside the box each time.

Teacher Share

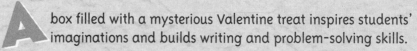

LANGUAGE ARTS

Valentine Treasure Box

A box filled with a mysterious Valentine treat inspires students' imaginations and builds writing and problem-solving skills.

◎ Wrap a box and lid with Valentine paper. (The size of the box should be just big enough to hold what's going inside.)

◎ Place a Valentine treat, or a coupon with clues that lead to the treat, inside the box. For example, if you're sharing heart-shaped cookies, you might provide directions students can follow to find the cookies. Pin the box to a bulletin board.

◎ Before Valentine's Day, invite children to write about what they think is inside the box and why. Encourage them to think about the size of the box as they make their guesses.

◎ Collect all guesses before February 14th. Reveal the contents on Valentine's Day and enjoy the surprise!

Mary Modoono
Shady Side Academy
Pittsburgh, Pennsylvania

TIP

In "Your Half, My Half," children find the missing halves of their hearts in books. For a special touch, hide the missing halves in books with Valentine's Day themes. Children will enjoy reading the books after performing the play.

LANGUAGE ARTS, MATH

"Your Half, My Half" Mini-Play

Students form two groups to perform a mini-play with a surprise ending! Divide the class into two groups: A and B. Have children in group A cut out and decorate hearts, one for every two students. Have them write a Valentine message on the hearts, then cut them in half to make puzzles. Have children in both groups practice their lines, then get ready to perform the play. Give children in group A one half of each heart. Place the other half of each heart in a book. When children in group B get to the part where they look for the missing half of each heart, let them search (with children in group A giving clues), then put the hearts they find together to read the messages. Children in group B can keep the hearts or present them to members of the audience. Switch the groups around (A is B, B is A) for a repeat performance so that everyone gets to make and receive a special valentine. Use the play to explore fractions: *How many halves in a whole?*

LANGUAGE ARTS

"Be Mine" Valentine Puzzles

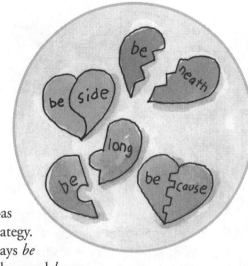

Looking for little words in big words is a strategy that helps young children read and write new words. Use a familiar Valentine message—*be mine*—as a springboard for strengthening this strategy. Share a conversation candy heart that says *be mine*. Read it with children and write the word *be* on the chalkboard. Spell it together, then ask children to listen for that sound in this word: *belong*. Ask them how they might spell the first part of that word (*be*). Write the word *belong* on the chalkboard so that children can see that the letters are the same. Now say three words—for example, *butter*, *behave*, and *bandage*—and ask children to identify the one that they think starts with the letters *be*. Follow up by giving children blank paper hearts. Have them write words that start with *be* on their hearts (such as *believe*, *before*, *begin*, *between*, *belong*, *beneath*, *beside*, *because*, and *beautiful*). Show students how to cut their hearts in half to make puzzles to share with one another.

Teacher Share

LANGUAGE ARTS, ART

Message in a Puzzle

These easy-to-make valentines are fun to put together and read. Write each child's name on separate slips of paper. Place the names in a bag. Let each child draw a name from the bag. Provide heart-shaped templates (big enough to write a message on). Have children trace and cut out a heart, then write a friendly message to their valentines. After decorating the hearts, have children cut them into puzzle pieces and place them in an envelope labeled with their valentine's name. Let children exchange these puzzles on Valentine's Day. What a great surprise when they put their puzzles together!

Lori Vig
Varnum Elementary School
Lowell, Massachusetts

TIP

You can easily adapt this activity to make a festive Valentine word wall. Cut out a large heart shape and write the words "Be mine" on it. Display this on a wall. Cut out smaller hearts in pinks and reds. Have children write words that start with the letters *be* on the hearts and add them to the display.

TIP

Valentine puzzles make nice, quick gifts for your students' special area teachers. Cut out giant puzzles for more fun, and have each child write a message on it.

TIP

To turn friendship rings into mini-books, remove staples, then place the strips one on top of another and staple along the left side to bind.

Teacher Share

Friendship Rings

These friendship rings grow each day as children write positive messages to each of their classmates. The rings are easily transformed into friendship books that children will cherish. (See tip, left.)

◎ Cut uniform strips of colored paper (about 12 by 3 inches). Give one to each child. Have children write their names on the strips and glue a small photo (or photocopy of a photo) next to their names.

◎ Show students how to staple the two ends together to form a ring (with the name and photo on the outside). String a clothesline across a wall and have children pin up their rings.

◎ Give each child a class list and a set of blank strips (one for each classmate). Beginning with the name that follows theirs on the class list, have children write a friendly message to each classmate, mentioning something positive about that child. Encourage them to be specific—for example, "I like the funny stories you tell about your dog." Have children sign their names, then locate the child's ring on the line, thread the strip through, and staple it to make a ring. Children will be excited to watch their friendship rings grow, until at last they can take them down and read them.

Sue Lorey
Grove Avenue School
Barrington, Illinois

Book Break

Saint Valentine
by Robert Sabuda (Atheneum, 1992)

Surprise! While we might associate roses with Valentine's Day, the *crocus* is actually the "official" flower of this holiday. Learn more about the history of this favorite February holiday with this exquisitely illustrated book.

MATH

Estimation Experts

A jar full of conversation hearts is just the thing to motivate a math lesson on estimation and counting skills.

◎ Fill a clear jar with candy hearts. Give each child a record sheet. (See sample, right.) Ask children to estimate how many hearts are in the jar and to record their guess in the first space.

◎ Take out about 1/4 of the candies (leaving the jar about 3/4 full) and count them with children. Put the candy back in the jar and let children revise their estimates if they wish.

◎ Repeat this procedure two more times. The last time, you will be removing about 3/4 of the candy hearts, counting them, and putting them back in.

◎ Conclude by counting all of the hearts in the jar. Let children compare each of their estimates with the actual number of hearts. *Which was their best? How close were they?* Encourage children to explain how they revised their estimates. Help them understand that estimates are not just random guesses. The more information they have about something, the better their estimates can be.

Name _____ Date _____

Estimation Experts

Estimate 1: _____ hearts

Estimate 2: _____ hearts

Estimate 3: _____ hearts

Estimate 4: _____ hearts

Estimate

1 2 3 4

was my best!
(circle one)

I guessed _____ hearts
too many/too few.

Teacher Share

SOCIAL STUDIES, LANGUAGE ARTS

Compliment Hearts

Explore concepts of friendship by making collaborative cards that children will read again and again.

◎ Let children each use a heart template to trace and cut out a large heart. Ask children to write their names in the center of the heart.

◎ Have children place their hearts on their desks, along with a few markers or colored pencils. Let children rotate to each classmate's desk and write a compliment on that child's heart.

By the end of this activity, each child will have a heart full of compliments—and a big boost in self-esteem!

Deirdre Parkhurst
Katonah Elementary School
Katonah, New York

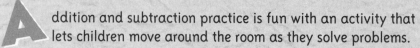

Teacher Share

(MATH)

Have a Heart

Addition and subtraction practice is fun with an activity that lets children move around the room as they solve problems.

◎ Make a set of heart-shaped cards. Write an addition or subtraction problem on one side of each heart. Write the answer or solution on the back of each heart. Label each heart (A, B, C, etc.).

◎ Make a grid, with boxes labeled A, B, C, and so on to match the hearts. Give a copy to each child.

◎ Place a heart on each child's desk. Have children start with that heart, solving the problem, then recording the answer on their grid and turning over the heart to self-check.

◎ At a designated signal, have children rotate to the next desk, solving that problem. Continue in this way until children have solved all of the problems.

Deirdre Parkhurst
Katonah Elementary School
Katonah, New York

SCIENCE, MATH, FITNESS

"A Big Heart" Calendar Activity

Ask children what they think it means to have a "big heart." (*to be especially kind, caring, and giving*) Ask children if they know how big their hearts are. Let them guess, then reveal that their hearts are about the size of their fists. Explain that the heart is a muscle and that, like other muscles in our bodies, we need to work at keeping it strong. Reinforce heart-healthy habits with this calendar activity.

◎ Give each child a heart-shaped card (with the fold at the top), sized to fit on a calendar square.

◎ On the inside of their hearts, have children write an exercise they can lead the class in. It can be silly or serious—for example, "Flap your arms like a bird for one minute." or "Do 20 jumping jacks, counting by twos." Have children sign their names to the outside of their hearts.

◎ Use a bit of removable wall adhesive to stick each heart to a calendar square. Write the date on each. When it's calendar time, let the designated child lift the flap and lead the class in a fitness activity!

Your Half, My Half

💚 A Fraction Valentine Play 💚

Characters Group A ♡ Group B

(A) Will you be my valentine?

(B) Yes, I think that would be fine!

(A) Then here's a heart for you to wear.

(B) But only half of it is here!

(A) Where can the other half be?

(B) Let's take a look around and see.

(A) What do we need? Where should we start?

(B) We need another half To make a whole heart.

(A) Is it underneath that chair?

(they search)

(B) No. It isn't anywhere!

(A) Let's look for it out in the hall.

(they look)

(B) It isn't anywhere at all.

(A) Could this square be the right part?

(finds and holds up a piece of paper)

(B) No, it wouldn't make a heart.

(A) Hey look!

(B) The pieces are hidden in that book!

(Hearts are in book. Children tape halves together.)

(A&B) Two halves make a whole. That's the end of our play. Have a happy Valentine's Day!

Fresh & Fun February   Scholastic Professional Books

TIP

As a variation, have children list as many things as they can that contain a particular president's name—for example, post chart paper labeled "Think'n Lincoln." Have children record places (Lincoln, Nebraska; the Lincoln Memorial), things (Lincoln Logs), and so on that share Abraham Lincoln's name.

Teacher Share

SOCIAL STUDIES

Presidential Places Scavenger Hunt

Strengthen map-reading skills and geography concepts, and spark students' interest in our country's leaders, with this ongoing activity. Display a large, detailed U.S. map at children's eye level. Post chart paper nearby and a list of all the presidents. Challenge children to locate and list as many places as they can that bear the name of a president. Have them record their findings on the chart paper and mark the spots on the map with small sticky-notes. (They can sign their names to the notes.)

Sue Lorey
Grove Avenue School
Barrington, Illinois

MATH, SOCIAL STUDIES

What Big Feet!

What do your students know about George Washington? They may know that he was the first president and that his picture is on a coin. But when they imagine him, do they see a man who was 6 feet 2 inches tall with size 13 feet? Bring in a pair of size 13 shoes. Let children trace around them, then take off their own shoes and step inside. Ask: *How long do you think Washington's feet were?* Measure them to find out. Then have children trace and measure their own feet. *How much bigger were Washington's?*

SOCIAL STUDIES, LANGUAGE ARTS

Mystery History

Spark students' interest in presidential history by posing a "Mystery History" challenge each day. Set up an eye-catching display area to post the challenge. Provide assorted resources for locating information, and a box for children to place their answers in. Sample Mystery History challenges include:

◎ Who was the tallest president?

◎ Which president was closest to your height?

◎ Name a president who was born in the state of [   ].

◎ What is the most common first name for a president?

MATH, SOCIAL STUDIES

Counting on Presidents

Strengthen math skills with an activity that connects money and presidents.

◉ Glue a picture of Abraham Lincoln to a paper plate and label it 1¢. Glue a picture of George Washington to a paper plate and label it 25¢.

◉ Place a quarter and a jar of pennies (more than 25) at a center along with the paper plates. Let children visit the center, inviting them to count out the number of pennies it takes to equal 25 cents and place them on the paper plate with Lincoln's picture.

◉ To vary the activity, cut out pictures of small toys or other items. Label the pictures with prices, such as 10¢, 15¢, and so on. Let children select pictures and count out the corresponding number of pennies. Or, have them count out pennies to make change from a quarter. Follow up by investigating other coins: *Whose picture is on a nickel? a half dollar? a dollar?*

Teacher Share

MATH

What Coin Am I?

Children find it interesting that different presidents are on U.S. coins. Let them learn more about presidents and money by making these self-checking riddle boards.

◉ Give pairs of children two sheets of 4- by 4-inch posterboard and two of the same coin. Have children examine their coins closely, noting as many details as they can.

◉ Have children write their facts in the form of clues on one sheet of posterboard, ending with "What coin am I?" Have them tape their coins—one heads-up, one tails-up—to the other sheet.

◉ Show children how to place the clues on top of the coins and then tape the top edges together. (The clues can then be lifted then to reveal the coins inside.)

◉ Display the riddles. Let students read the clues for different coins, guess what they are, and lift the flaps to see if they're right.

Bob Krech
Dutch Neck School
Princeton Junction, New Jersey

COMPUTER Connection

Take a tour of Lincoln's home and meet his family at these web sites:

....

showcase.netins.
net/web/
creative/lincoln/
gallery/pict.htm

....

www.geocities.
com/Sunset
Strip/Venue/
5217/lincoln.html

SOCIAL STUDIES, LANGUAGE ARTS

Abe and I Mini-Book

Abraham Lincoln's life was full of big changes—including going from living in a log cabin as a boy to living in the White House as president! What are some of the ways students' lives are different from Abe's life as a boy? Use pages 23 and 24 to make mini-books that compare everyday life then and now. Have students complete each mini-book page, then add a cover and bind.

Teacher Share

SOCIAL STUDIES, LANGUAGE ARTS

Stovepipe Hats

Surprise! Abe Lincoln kept notes stuffed in his stovepipe hat to remind him about important dates (and so he wouldn't lose the notes). Let children make their own stovepipe hats out of black construction paper. Have students tape notes about Abe to the outside of the hat. Let children wear their hats as they wander about the room, reading one another's facts. Follow up by letting each child share one new thing he or she learned.

Frank Murphy
Newton Elementary School
Newton, Pennsylvania

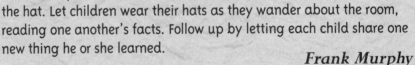

Book Break

Mr. Lincoln's Whiskers
by Karen Winnick (Boyds Mill, 1996)

Read about a young girl who wrote Lincoln to convince him to grow a beard. (He did!) After sharing this true story with students, you may find that they are inspired to make their own requests of the President. (See Computer Connection, left.) For more on the sixteenth president, share the anecdote-rich *Abe Lincoln's Hat* by Martha Brenner (Random House, 1994).

Book Break

The Legend of the Teddy Bear
by Frank Murphy (Sleeping Bear Press, 2000)

Did you know that one of our nation's presidents helped to give one of our country's most popular toys its name? Share this story to trace the history of the teddy bear and to discover more about Teddy Roosevelt, including his many pets (kangaroo rats, birds, dogs, squirrels, kittens, even a pony!).

Teacher Share

MATH, SOCIAL STUDIES

Design Your Own White House

Start by asking children if they know what the "White House" is. Share a picture of it and ask: *Why do you think it is called the White House?* Share a few more facts about this famous home—for example, some of the rooms are named after colors: There is a Green Room, Blue Room, and Red Room. One room is named after a shape: the Oval Office. Two bedrooms are named after people: the Lincoln Bedroom and the Queen's Bedroom. Let children design their own versions of the White House. Encourage them to show both interior and exterior views of the house and its rooms, and be sure they write or dictate labels for them. When finished, gather as a group and let children share their new visions for 1600 Pennsylvania Avenue!

Rita Galloway
Bonham Elementary School
Harlingen, Texas

Computer Connection

Tour the White House without leaving the classroom! Go to

www2.white house.gov/WH/ kids/html/ home.html

Book Break

Lives of the Presidents: Fame, Shame (and What the Neighbors Thought)
by Kathleen Krull (Harcourt Brace, 1998)

Which president enjoyed quilting? Which one weighed only 100 pounds? Who had two pet goats? Learn what the presidents were like in their everyday lives—what they ate, what they did for fun, and more.

TIP

Check for food allergies before letting children sample the snacks.

SNACK, SOCIAL STUDIES

Eat Like a President!

Plan a no-cook buffet to let children sample favorite foods of the presidents. Begin by asking: *What foods do you think a president might eat?* Some surprising presidential preferences have included turtle (Theodore Roosevelt), egg sandwiches (Franklin D. Roosevelt), and prune whip (Dwight D. Eisenhower). For no-cook presidential foods your students can help prepare, see the list that follows. (To learn more about presidents' favorite foods—and other things about their everyday lives—see Book Break, page 21.)

- Ulysses S. Grant liked cucumbers in vinegar for breakfast.
- Lyndon B. Johnson loved chipped beef and bread for breakfast.
- John Adams enjoyed cider.
- Richard Nixon was partial to pineapple rings with cottage cheese.
- Gerald R. Ford favored strawberries.
- Ronald Reagan's usual breakfast was bran cereal. He also enjoyed popcorn and, of course, jelly beans.

Teacher Share

TIP

Remember, because graphs are only as powerful as the discussions that go with them, be sure to ask questions to guide your students in examining the data they collect—for example, if you're graphing the states presidents were born in, you might ask: *How many more presidents were born in [state] than [state]?*

MATH, SOCIAL STUDIES

Graphing Presidents

After learning about presidents and their families, graph information to help students make comparisons and draw conclusions. (The type of graph you use will depend on the data gathered.) Ideas for graphing include:

- How many children did each president have?
- How many presidents were married when they were elected?
- How many presidents had a cat for a pet? a dog?
- How many presidents went to college?
- Which states were the presidents born in?

Jan Armstrong Freitag
Woodridge Elementary School
Bellevue, Washington

Abe lived in a log cabin with a dirt floor. It didn't have windows or running water.

①

I live in _____

_____

_____ .

Abe wore shirts made from a rough cloth called *linsey-woolsey*. He wore buckskin pants and a coonskin cap.

②

I wear _____

_____

_____ .

A^ctivity Page

Abe's mother cooked over a fireplace. His family grew vegetables. They went hunting for animals to eat. They made bread from cornmeal.

③

I eat food cooked _____

_____ .

My food comes from _____

_____ .

Abe helped his family by chopping wood for fires. He picked berries, nuts, and grapes to eat. He helped his father plant the garden.

④

I help *my family* by _____

_____

_____ .

Fresh & Fun February Scholastic Professional Books

Brush, Brush, Brush Your Teeth

February is Dental Health Month. And since it's also the month when children may be enjoying more sweets than usual in honor of Valentine's Day, why not plan a unit on teeth? Get started with an activity that will quickly and clearly demonstrate the benefits of brushing.

◎ Ask children why they think it's important to brush their teeth. Many will know that it's to prevent cavities. Ask: *Do you know how cavities can form in your teeth?* Explain that bacteria in our mouths change sugars in foods to acids. This causes a sticky substance called *plaque* to form on our teeth. Acids in the plaque attack tooth enamel (the outer layer of teeth), creating cavities. (Help children understand that lots of foods— not just candy—have sugars in them.)

◎ Fill two jars partway with vinegar. Tell children that the vinegar is like the acid in their mouths that can cause cavities. Place a raw egg in each jar. Explain that the eggshells are like their teeth.

◎ Remove one egg from the vinegar a few minutes after putting it in. Provide a toothbrush and toothpaste. Let children take turns gently brushing the egg and rinsing it. Set this egg on a paper towel. Explain that you will leave the other egg in the vinegar overnight. Ask: *What do you think we will see when we look at each egg tomorrow?* (The egg that was brushed and rinsed should be fine. The egg left in the vinegar will be pitted—like the cavities that form on teeth.)

Book Break

Grandpa's Teeth
by Rod Clement (HarperCollins, 1998)

Everyone's a suspect in this funny story about Grandpa and his missing false teeth. Follow up with a class "teeth hunt." Hide a handful of dried white beans (the teeth) around the classroom. Challenge children to find them all.

TIP

This is a good time to talk about flossing, too. Ask: *How do you think flossing helps prevent cavities?* (It helps remove food from between our teeth, preventing plaque from forming.)

Computer Connection

For more information about dental health, check these web sites:

www.ada.org

www.kidshealth.org

kidsdental.tsx.org

TIP

Primary teeth usually start to be replaced by permanent teeth by about six years of age. The front teeth are usually first to go. Primary teeth continue to be replaced by permanent teeth through about 13 years of age, at which time the 28 permanent teeth are usually in place.

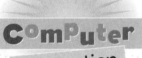

CoMPuter Connection

Track how many teeth children around the world lose with the Internet Schoolhouse:

www.internet schoolhouse.com

MATH

Tracking Teeth

How many teeth have your students lost? How do they think this compares to the number of teeth lost by another class in the same grade? by a class of younger students? older students? Conduct a survey to find out. Make copies of the tooth pattern here to gather data. Copy the pattern in a different color for each class that is participating in the survey. Have children write their names on the teeth and tell how many teeth they've lost. Use the markers to make a graph. Place the markers for each participating class side by side (above the number of teeth lost) to assist students in making comparisons. Use the graphs to guide a class discussion:

◎ How many children in our class have lost only one tooth? more than one tooth? no teeth?

◎ Have more children in our class lost at least one tooth or not lost any teeth?

◎ How does our class compare to the class of older students? younger students?

◎ About how many teeth do you think the average child your age has lost by now?

◎ How do you think this data might change at the end of the year?

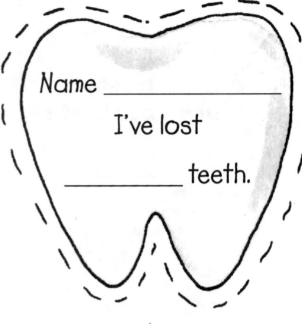

Name _____

I've lost

_____ teeth.

Tooth Pattern

Book Break

My Tooth Is About to Fall Out
by Grace Maccarone (Scholastic, 1995)

A young girl worries about where she will be when her first tooth falls out. Follow up by letting children write or dictate stories about where they were when their first tooth fell out (or where they think they might be when it happens). Give students tooth-shaped papers to write their final copies on.

Teacher Share

SCIENCE

Testing Teeth

Help children discover the strength of their teeth with a hands-on investigation. Divide the class into small groups. Give each group the following materials: a hammer; a rolling pin; a block of wood; four carrot sticks plus an extra carrot stick for each child in the group. Give each child a copy of the record sheet on page 29. Have children test the tools listed on the record sheet in order to see how well each works to grind up a carrot stick. Have them conclude the investigation by testing their own teeth as tools. Guide children in using the record sheet to rate the tools from one to five (five being the highest rating). Discuss what makes teeth such good tools for biting and chewing—for example, they're hard, sharp, and so on.

Natalie Vaughan
Phoenix School
Encinitas, California

LANGUAGE ARTS, ART, MATH

Collaborative Lift-the-Flap Banner

Give each child a copy of the banner template on page 30. Have them complete the rhyme for the animal of their choice, telling how many teeth the animal has on top, on the bottom, and in all. (Use the chart, right, for information.) Guide children in making the flap, cutting on the dashed lines and gluing the paper to another sheet of paper, being careful not to place glue on the flap or the area underneath. Have children draw and label a picture of their animal under the flap. Arrange papers side by side and tape together.

TIP

Check for food allergies before having children test their teeth as tools for grinding carrots.

TIP

Number of teeth on top, bottom, and in total follows (from left to right):

◎ fruit bat (12, 12, 24)
◎ hedgehog (20, 16, 36)
◎ guinea pig (10, 10, 20)
◎ kangaroo (18, 14, 32)
◎ giraffe (12, 20, 32)
◎ elephant (14, 12, 26)
◎ tiger (16, 14, 30)
◎ toucan (0, 0, 0)
◎ beaver (10, 10, 20)
◎ crocodile (30, 30, 60)
◎ hippopotamus (20, 18, 38)
◎ dog (20, 22, 42)

Throw Your Tooth on the Roof: Tooth Traditions From Around the World

by Selby B. Beeler (Houghton Mifflin, 1998)

What tooth traditions are your students familiar with? Many may know the Tooth Fairy. Invite them to share their stories, then read this book to introduce tooth traditions around the world. Follow up with "What Will the Tooth Fairy Leave?" (See below).

TIP

For more ideas and activities about teeth, see *Fresh & Fun: Teeth* by Jacqueline Clarke (Scholastic, 2000).

TIP

As a variation, let children play the part of the child and the Tooth Fairy. Tell them how many of each coin the Tooth Fairy is leaving. Have them place those coins under their pillows, then count them for a total.

MATH

What Will the Tooth Fairy Leave? Math Story Mat

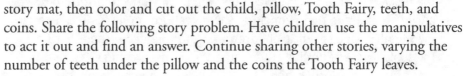

Invite the Tooth Fairy to visit your classroom with this math story mat activity. Give each child a copy of pages 31 and 32. Have children color the story mat, then color and cut out the child, pillow, Tooth Fairy, teeth, and coins. Share the following story problem. Have children use the manipulatives to act it out and find an answer. Continue sharing other stories, varying the number of teeth under the pillow and the coins the Tooth Fairy leaves.

How exciting! You just lost a tooth! It's time for bed. Be sure to place the tooth under your pillow before you go to sleep. (*Children place the tooth at the head of the bed, place the pillow on top, then put the cutout child into bed.*) What will the Tooth Fairy bring? Go to sleep or she won't come! (*Have children close their eyes. Visit each child's desk. Replace the tooth with coins, the same amount for each child.*) Wake up—it's morning! Time to look under your pillows. What did the Tooth Fairy bring? (*Have children look under their pillows and count the coins.*)

SCIENCE, MATH

What Big Teeth!

"What big teeth you have!" The story of Little Red Riding Hood has made an indelible impression on most of us as to the feeding habits of wolves. Are a wolf's teeth really as big and scary as this favorite fairy tale might have us believe? What animal does have the biggest teeth? Challenge children to find out. (They may be surprised to learn that an elephant's tusks are teeth (incisors), which make this animal's teeth the biggest of all—up to 10 1/2 feet long.) Build in more math by comparing the size of teeth. *How much bigger are an elephant's teeth than a child's teeth?*

Name _____ Date _____

Testing Teeth

How well did each tool grind up the carrot?
Rate the tools by circling a number from one to five.

	Hard to Grind				Easy to Grind
Hammer	1	2	3	4	5
Wood	1	2	3	4	5
Fingers	1	2	3	4	5
Rolling Pin	1	2	3	4	5
Teeth	1	2	3	4	5

◎ Which tool was most like your teeth? _____

◎ Name other foods that you can grind with your teeth.

_____

_____

Name _____ Date _____

Collaborative Lift-the-Flap Banner

What animal am I
with _____ teeth?
That's _____ on top
and _____ underneath!

Lift the flap
and you will see.
Who has more—
you or me?

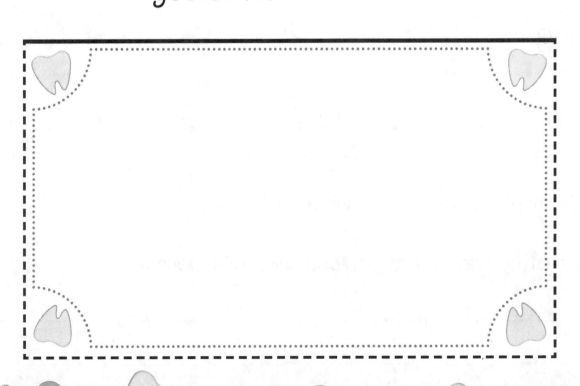

Fresh & Fun February Scholastic Professional Books

What Will the Tooth
Fairy Leave?
Math Story Mat

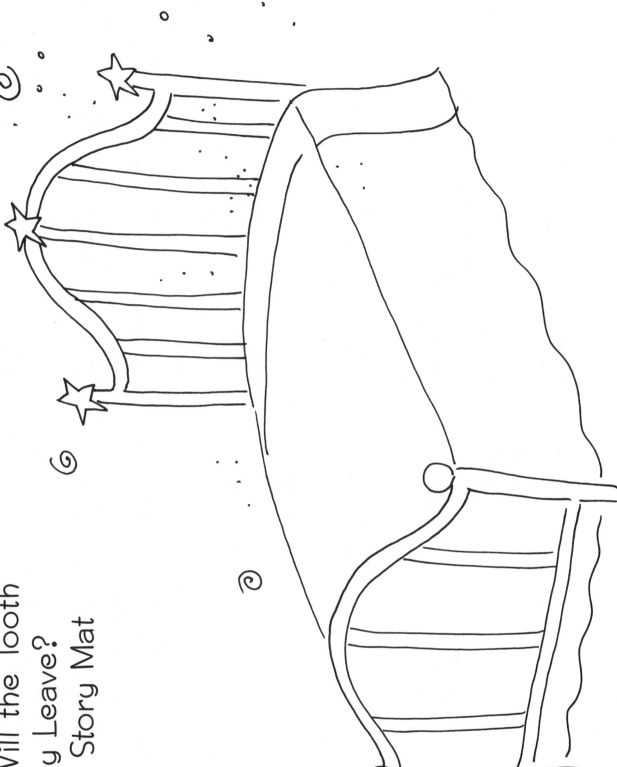

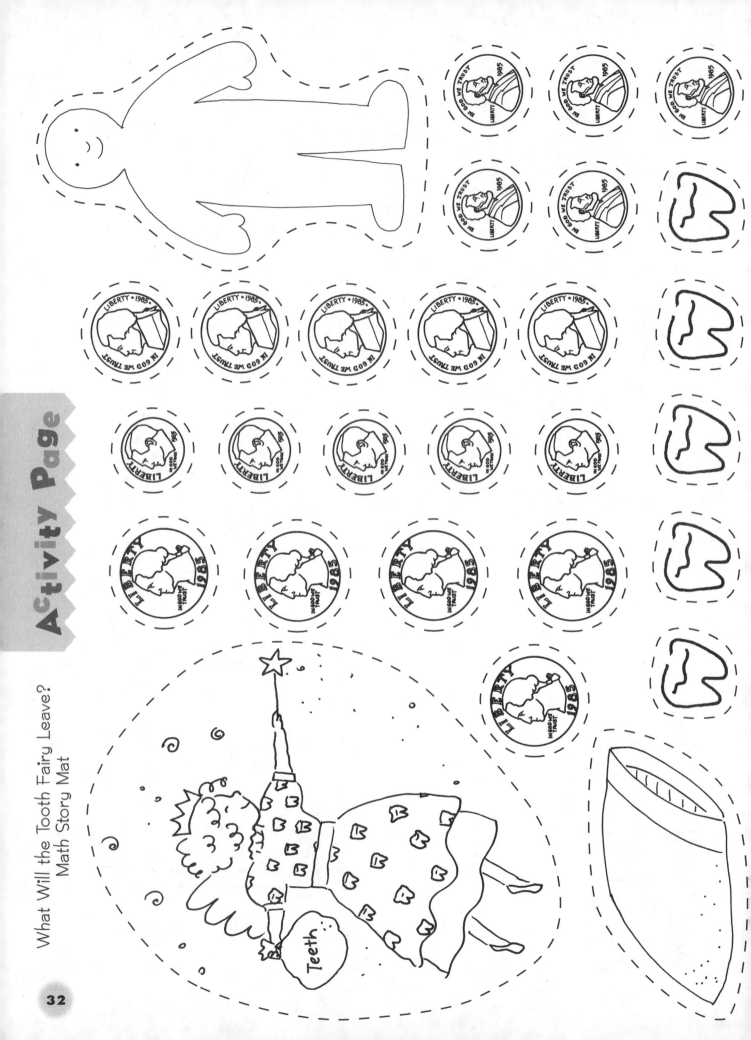

What Will the Tooth Fairy Leave?
Math Story Mat

Teeth